Let a Sorrowful Heart Sing

A Poetic Collection To Inspire Faith, Hope & Love

Cheryl L. Boone

Copyright © 2012 by Cheryl L Boone

Let a Sorrowful Heart Sing
by Cheryl L Boone

Printed in the United States of America

ISBN 9781619966314

All rights reserved solely by the author. The author guarantees all contents are original and do not infringe upon the legal rights of any other person or work. No part of this book may be reproduced in any form without the permission of the author. The views expressed in this book are not necessarily those of the publisher.

Unless otherwise indicated, Bible quotations are taken from the Nelson Study Bible, New King James Version. Copyright © 1979, 1980, 1982, 1997 by Thomas Nelson, Inc.

www.xulonpress.com

Dedication

First and foremost, I want to give praise to the Lord for giving me the inspiration to share what He has given. And for showing me a way to help others as He has helped me.

"Thank you" to my husband, Ken, for being so patient when I needed his shoulder, and for his silent pride and approval when I was so unsure.

Also, " thank you" to my mother, Lois, who has always shared in the excitement of each writing; my incredible daughter Shelli, and her wonderful husband Chris, who have given me the encouragement and support to pursue this endeavor; and to all my grand-children who gave me the reason.

It just wouldn't seem right not to mention certain people that the Lord used to "get through" to me. A very special "thank you" to my Aunt Angie, Aunt Carmen, my cousins Alice and Fede who gave me the extra "bit of advice" one very special day; my dear friends Chaplain Coston Charles, who gave me such wonderful advice and Adela, her husband and children who sealed the deal!

With all my love,

C.L.B

Table of Contents

Let a Sorrowful Heart Sing	*10*
The Beauty of You	*12*
A Rainbow for my Daughter	*14*
Oh, Lord, I Feel Lost	*16*
God's Secret Angel	*18*
The Precious Gift of Memories	*20*
Whispers in the Heart	*22*
It's Not a Total Mystery	*24*
Just a Little Prayer from You	*26*
And He Gave Us Flowers	*28*
My Heart Jumps for Joy	*30*
To My Best Friend, My Love	*32*
Our Little Angel	*34*
I'm a Different Person Now	*36*
Just Stay Focused on You	*38*
Isn't Life Funny	*40*
The Unwitting Example	*42*
The Seasons of Life	*44*
I'm Walking the Streets of Heaven	*46*
Oh, Lord, I'm Feeling Old Now	*48*
I've Fallen Short	*50*
Be Anxious for Nothing	*52*
Communication	*54*
When We Become One	*56*
A Truly Blessed Marriage	*58*
Thank You, Lord	*60*
Create In Me a Clean Heart	*62*
The Majesty of God's Great Love	*64*
Rain, Rain, Rain on Me Lord	*66*
Judge Not Lest Ye Be Judged	*68*
He Asked Me to Forgive	*70*
A Little Talk with God	*72*
Madison, You're God's Special Gift	*74*
And I Smelled Roses	*76*

Luke 10:27

"...You shall love the LORD your God with all your heart, with all your soul, with all your strength, and with all your mind, and your neighbor as yourself."

Help someone else in need and you'll find your heart overjoyed and your spirit at peace.

Let a Sorrowful Heart Sing

Lord, please use me
If only once I pray
Let me be of help to someone
Who's hurting inside today

I know that I'm not worthy
For you to work through me
But I have a willing heart
And I know that's all You need

There's someone out there needing You
Of that I can be sure
Maybe just a word or two
Would help them to endure

I don't need to know the reasons
You alone know all those things
Just use me Lord, to help someone
And let a sorrowful heart sing.

Psalm 50:1-2

"¹The Mighty One, God the LORD,
Has spoken and called the earth
From the rising of the sun to its going down,
²Out of Zion, the perfection of beauty, God will shine forth."

Give the Lord your praises every morning, noon and evening.
Praise Him for everything you are and everything He has
given you. Even God our Father rejoices to hear
accolades and thanksgiving!

The Beauty of You

I praise You, Lord
For this beautiful day
And give You thanks
For blessing me this way

The sky is so blue
And the sun is so bright
Your presence is all around
In this shining light

Help me to remember
That this day so new
Is a glorious reminder
Of the beauty of You

Genesis 9:13

"I set My rainbow in the cloud, and it shall be for the sign of the covenant between Me and the earth"

Have you ever taken the time to really savor the beauty of a rainbow? The absolute magnificence can't possibly be realized. The next time the Lord reminds us of His Covenant, take time to give thanks & praise.

Rainbow for My Daughter

Lord, I have a special favor
I'd like to ask of You today
You're the only one who can do it
That's why to You I pray

There's a special little blessing
It's not for me that I ask
But for my beautiful daughter
Are You willing to do the task?

It would take some brilliant colors
Red, yellow, blue and green,
With a swipe of Your hand across the sky
Make it look like an incredible dream

And when she sees this miracle
The sky colored in every hew
She'll forever keep it in her heart
'Cause she'll know it's a rainbow from you

Psalm 25:4-5

"⁴Show me Your ways, O LORD; Teach me Your paths, ⁵Lead me in Your truth and teach me, for You are the God of my salvation; On You I wait all the day."

There are always seasons in a person's life when there doesn't seem to be any focus or direction. Sometimes we don't know where we're going or how to get there. These are the times when we must recognize that it is Jesus that we need. It's Jesus we must call upon for help. Let Him have control of your life.

Oh, Lord I Feel Lost

Lord, please help me
To find my way
I can't help but feel
That I'm lost today

I'm not sure which direction
You want me to take
Can't depend on the decision
That I'm bound to make

Take control of my mind
My body and soul
Lead me to You, Lord,
I give You control

Matthew 6:4

".....that your charitable deed may be in secret; and your Father who sees in secret will Himself reward you openly."

⁓

Doing for others can be such a rewarding experience. Telling others about your good deed can only leave you with empty gratification and a braggart reputation.

God's Secret Angel

Sometimes, if you're very lucky
You may just get a peek
Of someone working incognito
To help someone else in need

You may never know it to look at them
But God's secret angel they are
Ready and willing to give to others
Never wanting to be the star

A gift beyond measure they'll issue
Leaving a memory in the heart
That will bring such joy and gratitude
It becomes an indelible mark

They're not looking for a thank-you
Or any recognition for the deed
They just want to share with another
The blessings they've received

This very special angel
Will be blessed a hundredfold
When the Lord announces in heaven
The gifts of love they've bestowed

Romans 1:8

"First, I thank my God through Jesus Christ for you all...."

*Take a moment to remember someone special and
say a little prayer for them.
Our prayers are remembered by our Lord eternally.*

Precious Gift of Memories

Oh, what a blessing to have someone special
Who's touched a part of your soul
A person of whom you respect and admire
A piece of your heart they hold

It might be something that they've said
Or something they always do
That's forever branded in your mind
And made an impression on you

A memory that brings a certain smile
Or a thought that brings a tear
Creates a picture in your mind
To hold that person near

Whether they be far away
Or living very close
Those precious memories in your mind
Are the gifts you treasure most

Proverbs 16:3

*"Commit your works to the LORD,
And your thoughts will be established"*

―――⁓―――

*The Lord doesn't speak in a loud voice to shock you into doing
His will, but will speak in a very gentle way to your heart.
It's your decision whether or not to listen.*

Whispers in the Heart

I heard some whispers in my heart
I wondered if they were from You
The thrill I felt inside myself
Helped me know that it was true

I know You've always loved me
But so far away I thought You were
Now it's me You're really talking to
Of that I can be sure

Never once could I ever imagine
That you would come to a person like me
And whisper in my heart
"I want you my servant to be"

Use my any way You can Lord
Let me give You my all and my best
With Your Spirit leading and guiding
I know You'll take care of the rest

Just help me keep my heart open
Pure, free and ready to give
Let those whispers be blessings to others
So to You they'll run and live

Psalms 118:8

*"It's better to trust in the LORD
Than to put confidence in man."*

―――◦〜―――

*The only way we can know the truth about the right way to live
is to read His holy book and know His Word.*

It's Not a Total Mystery

There is so much about this life
The Lord wants us to see
The beauty and the Glory of Him
Is there for you and me

It's not a total mystery
As we are given to believe
We've listened to the wrong source
And truly been deceived

The reality of Him is hidden
In plain sight if only we'll look
All the facts and information
God revealed to us in His Book

John 3:16

"For God so loved the world that He gave His only begotten Son, that whoever believes in Him should not perish but have everlasting life."

The Lord says that if we believe in Him we shall not parish.
Though we die in the flesh
our spirit shall spend eternity with Him.

Just a Little Prayer from You

I wish I could impress on you
The feelings I have inside
The pain that my heart feels
When from God I see you hide

The love for you I have
God alone can only share
Won't you just take a look
See what's waiting for your there

There are so many answers unfound
Until your heart's open to see
That all the pain you feel
Doesn't really have to be

Like a wall between you and Him
Sin has gotten in the way
But just a little prayer from you
Will take that wall away

I wish you would let me help
But all I can do is pray
That you'll set everything aside
And commune with Him this day

Matthew 6:28-29

"²⁸So why do you worry about clothing? Consider the lilies of the field, how they grow: they neither toil nor spin; ²⁹and yet I say to you that even Solomon in all his glory was not arrayed like one of these."

―――⤴―――

Take a little time to notice the beauty of a single flower and the wonder of it will uplift your heart.

And He Gave Us Flowers

How is it, Oh Lord
That you gave us flowers
With fragrance abundant
And beauty galore

While we ponder the Glory
And wonder in amazement
It's a glimpse of Your beauty
Our Father, we adore

1 Thessalonians 1:2

"We give thanks to God always for you all, making mention of you in our prayers..."

It's so exciting to catch a glimpse of the Lord in someone else's eyes. Sometimes, we even wish we could be as close to the Lord as we think they are. Just know that the Lord loves you just as much and is waiting to talk to you too!

My Heart Jumps for Joy

My heart jumps for joy
When in your eyes I see
The Spirit of the Lord
Showing from you to me

He's in your smile
And on your face
Everyone around will surely know
That because you've given Yourself to Him
The blessings through you flow

It's not always easy, His vessel to be
And you really can't fake the part
Truly, it's a blessing to me
To see Him in your heart

Song of Solomon 4:9

*"...You have ravished my heart
With one look of your eyes..."*

There's nothing more beautiful than the special bond that the Lord forms when two people give themselves to each other and to Him.

To My Best Friend, My Love

The sun is shining again in my life
Since you surrounded me with your love
You've sheltered me with your strength
Given you from above

It seems the Lord is directing our path
Removing all obstacles in our way
As long as the Lord is with us
Our love will be here to stay

This new life we'll be sharing
Is filled with excitement and elation
Together we can learn and grow
And build a strong foundation

God gave us the knowledge and wisdom
To keep our love in sight
We have the power to mold and shape
And create a beautiful life.

1 John 3:2

"Beloved, now we are children of God; and it has not yet been revealed what we shall be, but we know that when He is revealed, we shall be like Him, for we shall see Him as He is."

We don't know why the Lord may chose to take our child early, but we do have His word that we will be like Him and will obviously see our little one again.

Our Little Angel

You were our little Angel
So beautiful, so fare
Cute as a tiny button
With personality to spare

You always loved the Lord, Jesus
And to Him you would pray
Until one day He came along
And took our Angel away

Our hearts were truly broken
No words could ever express
How much to this day we miss you
And feel such emptiness

But our hope is still in Jesus
That we'll see you again one day
And together with our Lord in heaven
We will all eternally stay

2 Corinthians 5:17

"Therefore, if anyone is in Christ, he is a new creation; old things have passed away; behold all things have become new."

There is nothing on earth the same as being clean before our Lord; becoming new in Him. Confess your sins before the Lord and know that by His grace we are born anew in Him.

I'm a Different Person Now

I saw an old friend just recently
That I haven't seen in years
I wonder if she saw the change
And lack of all the fears

She didn't seem to notice
I wonder how that could be
I am a different person now
It's because of Jesus, I'm free

I hope I wasn't hiding it
To be the person she knew
It should have been so obvious
That my total life is new

Jesus died to make it happen
To give me eternal life
He gave me a new spirit
To glow in His bright Light

Now Jesus Christ is my Savior
And to His honor I live
I want everyone to know it
And to Him their praises give.

Matthew 6:33

"....but seek first the kingdom of God and His righteousness, and all these things shall be added to you."

―――⌒〜⌒―――

Just try putting the Lord first in your life and see the blessings He pours out on you.

Just Stay Focused on You

It seems to be so hard
To just stay focused on You
I'm constantly being attacked
No matter what I do

Temptation can always get to me
Especially when I am down
If I'd just keep my eyes on You
A life of peace would be found

As long as Your Spirit's within me
Your strength and power I'll have
Just keep my mind focused on You
And the circumstances won't seem so bad

Matthew 6:25

"Therefore, I say to you, do not worry about your life, what you will eat or what you will drink; nor about your body, what you will put on. Is not life more than food and the body more than clothing?"

Put the Lord first in all things and He will provide more than what you need.

Isn't Life Funny

Isn't life funny?
The way things work out
It's never how you want it
So you fuss and pout

Forethought it out
Gratification is in
Did you ever think
That it might be a sin?

Maybe a little prayer
And a talk with God
Can give you directions
You would never think of

Just tell Him you're sorry
And ask Him to forgive
You'll never have another doubt
About the right way to live

1 Timothy 4:16

"Take heed to yourself and to the doctrine. Continue in them, for in doing this you will save both yourself and those who hear you".

People notice the little things you do and say without you being aware. You never know how you touch others or whom you influence.

The Unwitting Example

Everyone sets an example
Whether it be good or bad
There is always a little someone
That you make happy or sad

Of course you're unsuspecting
That you're being watched that way
But a little someone is listening
To every word you say

A simple word or action
A little frown or big smile
Will become the seed that's nurturing
The thoughts of that little child

Then one day when that person is grown
With a character you've helped mold
They'll be an example to someone else
And your legacy they'll unfold

Job 42:2

"I know that You can do everything, and that no purpose of Yours can be withheld from You"

───⌒───

Job teaches us a lesson on patience. No matter how horrible circumstances were for Him, Job waited on the Lord and did not turn away or become angry with God. In the end, Job was blessed more than He could have ever imagined.

The Seasons of Life

The seasons you go through
Seem overwhelming at times
It's as if life itself
Has lost all rhyme

But appearances are deceiving
Circumstances can mislead
One step at a time
Is the attitude you need

If your focus is on God
When all seems against you
Your faith and His strength
Will surely see you through

Revelation 21:21

"The twelve gates were twelve pearls: each individual gate was of one pearl. And the street of the city was pure gold, like transparent glass"

According to God's word, the colors and the scene in heaven is more spectacular than we could ever imagine. Oh, what glory awaits us!

I'm Walking the Streets of Heaven

I'm walking the streets of Heaven
And, oh, what a glorious path
I'm hand in hand with Jesus
And truly home at last

The streets are really golden here
And the colors so pure and clean
I'm alive as I've never known it
Heaven's really an incredible scene

Don't be concerned or worried
I'm smiling from ear to ear
Filled with happiness unknown before
And excited that I'm here

I know you're a little frightened
Especially from your point of view
But I'm in the hands of the Lord now
And we'll always be there with you

I wish that you could see this with me
But we each have to take our own path
Just know in your heart I still love you
Nothing could ever change that fact

Someday we'll share this together
And you'll know the happiness I feel
Until then, my loved ones, remember
That the life Jesus gives is real!

Matthew 11:28-30

*"²⁸Come to Me, all you who labor and are heavy laden,
and I will give you rest.
²⁹Take My yoke upon you and learn from Me, for I am gentle
and lowly in heart, and you will find rest for your souls.
³⁰For My yoke is easy and My burden is light".*

---

*Sometime the pain of life itself becomes a burden too hard to bear.
Just remember how the Lord suffered for you. Give all your pain
and fears to Him. As long as you are alive He will use you
for some purpose possibly unknown to you.*

Oh, Lord, I'm Feeling Old Now

Oh, Lord, I'm feeling old now
My body's in so much pain
I can't seem to move like I use to
I don't really want to complain

But along with a body I can't handle
Are mental apprehension and fears
Please always stay close, guide me
And comfort me through the tears

Sometimes it can be so frightening
Being doubtful where I stand
Compared to Jesus I'm not worthy
But You've offered a saving plan

I know if I'll say I'm sorry
And accept Jesus as my King
The Life He gave for my sins
Will cause the Angles to sing

Lord, now I know where I'm headed
Straight into Your arms to stay
But for now Lord, I'll be contented
To savor each and every day

Romans 3:23

"for all have sinned and fall short of the glory of God…"

---

*We must not measure how good we are against other people,
but against how good Jesus is.
He is perfect but we have all sinned. Praise be to Jesus
who paid the price for our sins.*

I've Fallen Short

"All have sinned and fallen short"
Are the words I often here
But looking at others who are really bad
My way seems pretty clear

I try to be good and do for others
And surely when being compared
The Lord will accept me as I am
My place in heaven is prepared

But God also said that I'm not righteous
I wonder what he could have meant
I know deep inside that I have sinned
Maybe I'm not heaven bent

My Lord gave His Son who gave His Life
Now I know there's a way for me
If I'd just admit how bad I am
I can live with Him eternally

Though I may be deceived about some things
God's Word says one thing is true
That the only way we'll get to heaven
Is through "Jesus" for me and you

Philippians 4:6

"Be anxious for nothing, but in everything by prayer and supplication, with thanksgiving, let your requests be made known to God..."

*When you're worried and uncertain which direction
to take or what to do,
take some time to tell the Lord your fears.
He has promised to give you peace
beyond all understanding. Just let Him do it.*

Be Anxious for Nothing

There are times in my life
When the seasons are cold
I worry and worry
But no answers unfold

My prayers to the Lord
Seem almost in vain
I've tried everything I know
To stop this awful pain

Then one day I read
In His Word so divine
"Be anxious for nothing"
Be still and let Him shine

The lessons He's givng me
Will show of His love
Be still and listen
There are miracles above

Psalm 19:14

"Let the words of my mouth and the meditation of my heart be acceptable in Your sight, O LORD, my strength and my Redeemer"

Relationships are built and destroyed by communiciation. Better to become a great listener than to become known for your debating talents.

Communication

Communication if difficult
You'll hear people say
I think it's impossible
In the world today

For some strange reason
The words you mean
Are heard by another
As something obscene

It's perfectly simple
In your mind you feel
But to someone else
It's something unreal

It's as if two languages
Are being spoken
With lack of understanding
Communication is broken

Maybe it's prudent
To take some advise
Take time to listen
And before speaking think twice

Hebrews 13:4-5

"⁴Marriage is honorable among all, and the bed undefiled:...
⁵Let your conduct be without covetousness, and be content with
such things as you have, for He Himself has said,
"I will never leave you nor forsake you".

Nothing is more important than keeping your eyes on
the Lord and your spouse first.
Focusing on what you don't have or what you're not getting,
will inevitably lead you to unhappiness.

When We Become One

When we become one with joy in our hearts
A bond of love is formed at the start
The Lord looks upon us and seals this bond
Bestows a blessing to help us go on

A blessing of commitment, courage and strength
To fight life battles each day of the week
Together we'll stand side by side as one
Growing closer every moment that life goes on

The focus on each other must stay just that way
For looking at ourselves will turn us astray
But keeping the Lord with us joins not two but three
And we'll have the strongest love and true unity

The mountains will be there but never too high to climb
And the Lord will be with us when one day we'll find
That this marriage God blessed in the beginning to true
Has been a blessing to others as together we grew

1 Corinthians 13:4-7

"Love suffers long and is kind; love does not envy; love does not parade itself, is not puffed up; does not behave rudely, does not seek its own, is not provoked, thinks no evil; does not rejoice in iniquity, but rejoices in the truth; bears all things, believes all things, hopes all things, endures all things."

A truly blessed marriage doesn't just happen. It takes love, patience, commitment and focus on the other person before self. Without the Lord's help it is impossible.

A Truly Blessed Marriage

It will never be forgotten
The day that you were wed
There were tears in your eyes
As your vows you said

A little frightened and anxious
About what was to be
But trusting in God
That your life He would lead

Now all these years later
It's obvious to see
That together with God
You've found true unity.

Psalm 100:4

"Enter into His gates with thanksgiving, and into His courts with praise. Be thankful to him and bless His name."

When you love someone, you'll be the first to stand and applaud them; and the last one to condemn them. Thank you Jesus for standing by me every day!

Thank You, Lord

Thank You, Lord
For all that You've given me
There's not a single thing in my life
That wasn't always meant to be

There have been some times of grieving
And times that I'll always treasure
Times when I was so confused
Times of joy beyond measure

Even when I rebelled in life
You patiently waited for me
You knew all along I'd come back to You
Your Son in my life I'd need

Now I thank You again, my Father
For keeping me always in sight
And showing me by Your Holy Spirit
How to live this beautiful life

Psalm 51:10

*"Create in me a clean heart, O God,
And renew a steadfast spirit within me."*

―――∽―――

Psalm 51 has always been where I run to when sin builds the wall between me and the Lord.

Create In Me a Clean Heart

Oh Lord, show me your tender mercy
I know my sins before You are great
Can't carry this burden within me
My heart from within does ache

I know you gave Your Son
Who shed His blood for me
That I would be made clean
From sin You set me free

Create in me a clean heart
This prayer I say each day
Let my lips shout Your praises
Let me teach others Your ways

Restore my joy in Your salvation
Let Your Spirit within me reside
He'll guide me to do Your will
So the incense of my praises will rise

Genesis 1:31

"God saw all that He had made, and indeed it was very good."

~~~~~

*Recently, during an airline flight, I stared out the window and
I marveled at the beauty and spectacle of what I saw.
This poem was written during that flight.*

The Majesty of God's Great Love

High above the ice capped mountains
Souring on the wings of a dove
As far as my eyes can wander
Is the majesty of God's great love

The gleaming sun sparkling on the water
Far below as I glide so high
Pillows of clouds dotted here and there
As I search the length of a turquoise sky

There is no understanding
Of the beginning or the end
There's just the sense of knowing
What my mind can't comprehend

That my God created this beauty
For all of us to share
And know this is just the beginning
Of what waits for us there

Hosea 10:12

*"Sow for yourselves righteousness; Reap in mercy;
Break up your fallow ground,
For it is time to seek the LORD, Till He comes and
rains righteousness on you."*

---

*When we repent of our sins
we allow the Lord to rain blessings on us.*

Rain, Rain, Rain on Me Lord

Rain, rain, rain on me, Lord
Let your cleansing Spirit flow,
I'm so dirty from my sins
It weighs heavy on my soul

Rain, rain, rain on me, Lord
Find my innermost thoughts that hide
Cleanse me from head to toe
Let no spot remain inside

My sins seem thick, ugly as grime
I get lost in the mucky mire
It won't allow Your light to shine
Won't let my thoughts go higher

Rain, rain, rain on me, Lord
Let your cleansing spirit flow
Cover me with His atoning blood
And in your eyes I'll be white as snow

Matthew 7:1

"Judge not, that you be not judged"

---

*It seems easy to see the faults and sins of others.
The truth is that when we come before the Lord,
it won't be their sins that will concern us.*

Judge not Lest Ye Be Judged

I learned a special lesson today
From a very dear old friend
Although she didn't know it
She showed a heart that wouldn't bend

I always though she was closer to God
Than I could ever be
But in just a single act
I saw her no better than me

It's easy to say someone's selfish
Or get angry at something they've said
But we really don't know what they're going through
Or the emotions and feelings in their head

It's easy to forget how sinful we are
When in our heart we're holding a grudge
We all suffer affects of our own sins
So "Judge not lest ye be judged"

Luke 6:37

"...forgive, and you will be forgiven"

As the Word says, it's easy to forgive someone when it doesn't really mean anything to you in the first place. But try to forgive someone who has inflicted pain that pierces the core of your being. Whenever you think it's too hard...remember Jesus on the cross. Think about the forgiveness He gave.

He Asked Me to Forgive

One day the Lord asked me
To do something special
And I proudly accepted the task

Just lead me and guide me
I'm anxious to be used
"I'll do anything that You ask"

I guess He took me at my word
And didn't hesitate to say
The first thing I want you to do for Me
Is to forgive ALL this very day

He was sure to point out
I could hold nothing back
Revenge was ultimately His

But wouldn't you know…
Of all the jobs on earth
He would ask me to forgive

Matt 5:4

"Blessed are those who mourn, for they shall be comforted."

Only the imagination can hear the potential conversation that a believer may have with the Lord prior to passing on to their beautiful new life.

A Little Talk With God

Dear Lord, please help us
We just have to know
Why did Wilma leave us;
Why did she go?

I fancied I heard God
Answer this way,
Telling me why
She didn't have to stay…

"I came upon Wilma
Struggling with life
Trying to hold on
To a body in strife

I reached out My hand
And said, "Come with Me"
There is another world
I want you to see.

It's a world without pain
Sorrow or sin;
A world full of beauty
And peace within".

"But Lord, just a minute
I can't go just yet…
I have a family
I just can't forget"

"Trust in Me, Wilma
And I'll promise you this day
I'll always take care of them
While you're away."

I know they'll miss you
And feel lonely at times,
But I'll be there to lean on
When they feel like crying.

I promise you I'll be there
To wipe each tear
Giving them comfort
When they feel fear.

And when they think of you
With love in their hearts,
I'll give them a special touch
And enfold them in My arms".

"OK, Lord I'm ready
To entrust them to You
You are the only One
Who could love them as I do".

"So Wilma made the decision
To come along with Me,
Knowing her love
Will encompass you eternally".

Psalm 127:3

"children are a heritage from the LORD, The fruit of the womb is a reward"

The sweet spirit of this young lady is a blessing to all who know her. She is a special gift of the Lord.

Madison, You're God's Special Gift

The day you were born
It was sure you were to be
A very special little gift from Him
Who would change the world for me

A little cross on your forehead
And a kiss from the Lord above
Was just God's way of beginning
This new precious life we love

He chose the perfect parents
To guide and protect your way
And teach you of God's great gift
That you could receive some day

Now you've become a young lady
And the love of Jesus you've found
Accepted Him as your savior
You're baptized and heaven bound

Your eyes show God's sweet spirit
Compassion is your whole being
It's obvious to all around you
It's Jesus in you they're seeing

Thank you, my precious Madison
For accepting Jesus this way
And showing everyone around you
What heaven will be like someday

He held Jesus' hand as he let go of mine!

*There is nothing more precious,
more heart wrenching, more bewildering, more extraordinary
than being a part of the most miraculous moment in a person's life:
their journey from this world into their real home in eternity.*

In Memory of my Daddy
Tony Rottino

Born into this world and life
On March 28, 1921

Born into his true life for eternity
On June 22, 2010

His journey here is now over.
He's home with his family!
He is, for the first time ever, truly happy!

And I Smelled Roses

I wonder if you could imagine
The emotions I felt that night
When Jesus came and took dad's hand
While I sat by his side

I knew that he was leaving
So praying was all I could do
Reading scripture and thinking
Wondering now what the Lord would do

I sat by his bed with my arms out stretched
My head bowed in contemplative thought
Not knowing what I could possibly do
The Lord's directions is all I sought

I wondered what dad was feeling
As I stared at him for so long
He seemed to be so peaceful
Sleeping sound and very calm

Wondering what would happen next
I sat and pondered these things
Lord, please be with him now
Oh, let his heart joyously sing

Then all of a sudden I saw something
No words could explain what it was
But later that evening while reflecting
I knew it was dad's leaving I saw

And as I arose to cradle his head
Before I could take it all in
The fragrance of roses filled the air
I knew Jesus was there with him.

A Special "Thank You" to you the reader...

So many times in my life I've had experiences when I just knew that "Someone was watching over me". Some things in life just can't be explained, but you know when you've been touched in such a way that makes an impression on your life. I pray you've been blessed in some small way that will make a difference to you.

Please remember "JESUS" is the name above all names. No other name under heaven can answer your prayers and bless your life.

I truly thank you for taking time to read this little book and I hope that I have helped to

Let a Sorrowful Heart Sing

Cheryl L Boone

Somewhere
in this little book is a hidden message meant for someone in need at this very moment.

Somehow
this message will find its way into the hands of that one person that the Lord wants to encourage and bless!

It seems that in this life everyone has their trials, tribulations and life lessons that the Lord sets before you. If you want to be used of the Lord, then you must listen, learn and take a step of faith.

For Cheryl, it seemed that every experience in her life somehow worked together to bring her to this place. Looking back, she could see that the Lord orchestrated every experience to work for her good.

Along the way, through difficult times and exciting times, she had questions that weighed heavy with emotion. While sitting at a kitchen counter one day during one of these times, pen and paper in hand, she started writing to the Lord. By the time she came to the end she had an answer. Though the writings were personal it became evident that the Lord used these writings to help others who could relate to the circumstance. It was through these writings that lessons have been learned.

Though encouraged by her daughter and family to share these writings there was always something that held her back. Then just at that perfect moment a friend told her how one of her poems had helped someone who was hurting.

Someway
the Lord will use this book to
Let a Sorrowful Heart Sing!

CPSIA information can be obtained at www.ICGtesting.com
Printed in the USA
LVOW060402070312

271900LV00002B/31/P